Spotlight on Kids Can Code

Understanding Coding with
APPLE SWIFT

Michael Riccio

PowerKiDS press
New York

Published in 2018 by The Rosen Publishing Group, Inc.
29 East 21st Street, New York, NY 10010

Copyright © 2018 by The Rosen Publishing Group, Inc.

All rights reserved. No part of this book may be reproduced in any form without permission in writing from the publisher, except by a reviewer.

First Edition

Editor: Theresa Morlock
Book Design: Michael J. Flynn

Photo Credits: Cover Gary John Norman/Cultura/Getty Images; pp. 5, 11 vgajic/E+/Getty Images; p. 7 ronstik/Shutterstock.com; p. 8 Kaspars Grinvalds/Shutterstock.com; p. 13 JGI/Tom Grill/Blend Images/Getty Images; p. 15 Hero Images/Getty Images; p. 19 Prostock-studio/Shutterstock.com; p. 21 goodluz/Shutterstock.com.

Cataloging-in-Publication Data

Names: Riccio, Michael.
Title: Understanding coding with Apple Swift / Michael Riccio.
Description: New York : PowerKids Press, 2018. | Series: Spotlight on kids can code | Includes index.
Identifiers: ISBN 9781508156024 (pbk.) | ISBN 9781508155157 (library bound) | ISBN 9781508154808 (6 pack)
Subjects: LCSH: Swift (Computer program language)–Juvenile literature. | Application software–Development--Juvenile literature.
Classification: LCC QA76.73.S95 R53 2018 | DDC 004.1675–dc23

Manufactured in the United States of America

CPSIA Compliance Information: Batch #BS17PK: For Further Information contact Rosen Publishing, New York, New York at 1-800-237-9932

Contents

What's Apple Swift?......................4
Basic Programming........................6
Getting Started..........................8
The Rules of Coding.....................10
"Hello, World"..........................12
Getting More Complicated................14
You Already Know Coding Language........16
Asking the "App"ropriate Questions......18
Are These Apps?.........................20
You're on Your Way......................22
Glossary................................23
Index...................................24
Websites................................24

What's Apple Swift?

There are many coding languages in the programming world. Every language has a different name. In fact, you may have already heard of some of them, including Java, Ruby, Python, or Objective-C. There are hundreds of programming languages, and each is different from the others.

In 2014, Apple Inc. released a new coding language called Swift to replace its old language. The company wanted a language that was simple enough to save programmers time and easy enough for new users to learn. One helpful thing about Swift is that it has the ability to infer what a user means in their code. This means that the program can figure out what someone is trying to say without being specifically told. This makes Swift smarter than older coding languages and means there's less code to learn.

Newer coding languages, such as Swift, usually build on older languages. Swift is based on many different coding languages, so it shares many words with these other languages.

Basic Programming

When you open an **application** on any device, you usually see the **graphical user interface** or GUI (GOO-ee) for short. A GUI uses pictures, sometimes called graphics, instead of showing you lines of code. A GUI also serves as a shortcut for the user, so when you make changes in the program, you don't have to update any code yourself.

Behind the scenes are thousands of lines of code, which we can also call instructions. This code is telling the computer what steps to take for each user action. Every picture, button, text box, and item has code working in the background. Some code can be very simple and some code is more difficult, but a program can't run unless there is code to tell it how to run and what to do.

Your computer reads, understands, and reacts to thousands of lines of code in microseconds.

Getting Started

Apple Swift was developed just for programming on Apple devices. You can only write code with Apple Swift on an Apple computer or Apple device. Apps created with Swift will only work on Apple devices.

However, Swift uses many common programming words. If you can learn the most basic terms in Swift, you'll be able to use those words and ideas with other coding languages. Here are some of the most common programming words we'll see in Swift.

MacBook

Some types of coding language aren't very different from normal speech. Once you know a few words, you can read code like you would read a book.

Var: Short for the word "variable," which is a quantity that may change when other conditions change. (Example: x=5 or dog=10)

Let: Creates a constant in our code. A constant is something that can't be changed.

String: A group of letters or numbers.

Boolean: A variable with two possible values called "true" and "false."

Function: A section of code that performs a task.

Breaking the Code

To code using Swift, you will need an Apple device, such as a MacBook, with an operating system of OS X 10.9 or higher. This computer will have the program Xcode, in which you can begin writing your first programs.

The Rules of Coding

Learning a coding language like Swift is only the first step toward making your first app. The next step is having an idea. Without a plan, even the best coder won't have anywhere to go. First, let's go over some rules of coding. If you follow these rules, you'll be on your way to building your first app.

Rule 1: Coders must know what they want the computer to do and write a plan.

Rule 2: Coders must use special words to have the computer accept `input`, make choices, and take action.

Rule 3: Coders need to think about what tasks can be put into a group.

Rule 4: Coders need to employ `logic` using AND, OR, NOT, and other key words.

Rule 5: Coders must explore the `environment` and understand how it works.

When you start to build your app, it's okay to make changes to your plan. Keep a notepad by your side so you can write down your steps.

"Hello, World"

Here we go! Let's write our first line of code. The first program most programmers write in any language is the "Hello, world" program. This is a simple program that will show you some basic skills.

We'll start with a print command, which tells the computer to display whatever comes next. We then add parentheses so our program knows where to start and stop. Last, we type out our string between the parentheses.

```
1   Print ("Hello, world")
```

That's it! This is an entire program in Swift. Run that code by hitting enter and see what happens.

Earlier we said that Swift can infer what you are trying to do. In this program, Swift knows that we're trying to display a string because of the quotation marks. If you're using a string, the computer will run the command and display exactly what you wrote in those quotation marks.

"Display" has many meanings. It can mean to show something. It can also mean a monitor. Your computer monitor is a display because it can show text such as "Hello, world."

Getting More Complicated

Let's take some of the commands from earlier and talk about how those are used in Swift. Here we'll use constants, which we can use by typing "Let" followed by a space and the letter A or B.

```
1   Let A="Hello"
2   Let B="world"
3   Print(A + ", " + B)
```

When we use a constant, we take a letter such as A and pair it with something else. Above we have A="hello" and B="world." In the third line, we're using the same print command from last chapter, but this time we put in our constants instead of words.

When we **execute**, or run, the last line of code, we're telling Swift to combine A and B into the same line. Since A is actually the word "Hello" and B is actually the word "world," we end up with:

```
4   \\Hello, world
```

You can think of a constant as a shortcut. If you have to repeat the same phrase multiple times in your code, it's much easier to use a constant.

15

You Already Know Coding Language

The symbols we use in math, such as the addition (+) and subtraction (-) symbols, are all commands in Swift. Swift also recognizes numbers. Whole numbers, such as 1 or 3, are called **integers**. You can use integers and these symbols in the same way you would on paper.

The code below is a simple program that adds the variables X and Y. It's important that we use variables because we're going to change this program in a moment.

```
1   Var X=1
2   Var Y=3
3   Print (X+Y)
4   \\4
```

Swift also can do multiplication (*) and division (/). Try changing the variables around and see if you can build a calculator app.

There is a second type of number in Swift. These numbers are called doubles. Doubles are similar to integers, but they have a decimal point. Here's the same program above, this time using doubles.

```
5   X=1.0
6   Y=3.0
7   Print(X+Y)
8   \\4.0
```

Line 8 is a double because Swift will infer that we're working with doubles when it sees the decimal point.

Breaking the Code

Lines 1 through 8 are all part of the same program. After the variable is defined in line 1, Swift will remember that the letter X is a variable. From now on in this program you just write "X=" and the new number to change that variable.

Asking the "App"ropriate Questions

A Boolean is a variable that can either be true or false. A Boolean usually has an if-else statement. An if-else statement is an action and a reaction. The "if" is the user's action. The "else" is what happens after the user's action. For example:

```
1   var Horses=5
2   var Pigs=3
3   if Horses == Pigs{
4   print("You have the same number of Pigs and Horses")}
5   else{
6   print("The number of Pigs and Horses is different")}
```

"Horses" and "Pigs" are two variables that represent animals. There are five horses and three pigs. Our program wants to know if we have the same number of pigs and horses. If we do, then it prints one string. If we don't, it prints another string.

You may have noticed there are two equal signs between Horses and Pigs. This is our Boolean. Writing "==" asks if the variables are **identical**. Since 3 and 5 are not equal, the program returns the "else" statement.

Other Booleans include less than (<), greater than (>), and not equal to (!=). How could we use these to change our program?

Are These Apps?

An app doesn't need to be **complicated**, it just needs to perform a specific task. However, programming takes time, and the code behind the apps you use can be very complicated. So, let's learn one final piece of code to bring everything together.

Functions are sections of code that complete a task. Functions are written with many of the pieces of code we've already used. We'll start with the beginning of a grocery list function:

```
1  func ShoppingList(Food: String) -> String{
2  let Item = "Buy " + Food + "."
3  return Item}
```

This code starts with a new term, "func," which is short for function. After a space, we can now name our function: ShoppingList. Inside ShoppingList, we're going to store "Food," and we need to tell Swift that "Food" is a string value. Then we see an arrow.

The arrow means return, or in this case, display. If we repeat this code, but replace "String" with "Apples," the return arrow tells the computer what to do next. Look at our final **output** to see for yourself.

```
4    Print (ShoppingList(Food: "Apples"))
5    \\ Buy Apples.
```

Apps will have multiple functions and sometimes even functions inside of functions. Learning how to write a function will unlock the doors to bigger projects in Swift.

You're on Your Way

To build bigger projects, you'll need to build bigger code with more complicated language. But never forget that everything in Swift is part of the English language. If you come across a new command you don't understand, it sometimes helps to think about the word's definition outside of Swift.

Also remember that a lot of learning comes from making mistakes. Don't be afraid to try different code, and don't give up if you feel **frustrated**. Code can always be fixed. No program is perfect the first time it's written. Professional programs take months and sometimes years of editing before they're completed. Even the creators of the most popular programs are always updating or fixing problems they didn't know existed before.

Now that you have a basic understanding of Swift, your journey is just beginning. Make a plan and execute that code!

Glossary

application: A program that performs one of the tasks for which a computer, smartphone, or tablet is used.

complicated: Hard to understand.

environment: The combination of computer hardware and software that allows a user to perform various tasks.

execute: Carry out or perform a task.

frustrated: Feeling upset or discouraged.

graphical user interface: The picture-based display that a user sees and works with.

identical: Exactly the same.

input: Information that's entered into a computer.

integer: A whole number, such as 2 or 42.

logic: The steps of thought used to solve or understand a problem.

output: The information that a computer produces by processing a specific input.

Index

A
application (app), 6, 8, 10, 11, 16, 20

B
Boolean, 9, 18, 19

C
coding languages, 4, 5, 8, 9, 10, 16
commands, 12, 14, 16, 22
constant, 9, 14, 15

D
doubles, 17

E
environment, 10

F
function, 9, 20, 21

G
graphical user interface (GUI), 6

I
if-else statement, 18
input, 10
integers, 16, 17

J
Java, 4

L
logic, 10

M
MacBook, 8, 9

O
Objective-C, 4
output, 21

P
Python, 4

R
Ruby, 4

S
string, 9, 12, 18, 20

V
variable, 9, 16, 17, 18

X
Xcode, 9

Websites

Due to the changing nature of Internet links, PowerKids Press has developed an online list of websites related to the subject of this book. This site is updated regularly. Please use this link to access the list: www.powerkidslinks.com/skcc/swift